GW00493564

Name _____
School _____
Class _____

Pronuniciation Guide (IPA) 讀音指南 (國際音標)

Consonants 輔音		
Symbol 符號	Example 例子	
p	pen	cup
b	boy	job
t	tea	cut
d	dog	bad
k	cold	look
g	get	big
tʃ	chair	lunch
dʒ	jam	fridge
f	four	off
v	vase	give
θ	thin	bath
ð	this	breathe
s	say	face
z	zoo	nose
ʃ	she	wash
ʒ	leisure	treasure
h	hat	how
m	make	arm
n	neck	fan
ŋ	sing	long
l	lamp	doll
r	red	run
j	year	you
w	we	wind

Vowels 元音		
Symbol 符號	Example 例子	
iː	sea	sheep
ɪ	pig	sit
e	leg	ten
æ	cat	man
ɑː	car	glass
ɒ	box	hot
ɔː	ball	short
ʊ	book	put
uː	do	shoe
ʌ	cup	sun
ɜː	bird	word
ə	again	butter
eɪ	cake	name
əʊ	go	home
aɪ	five	my
aʊ	cow	house
ɔɪ	boy	noise
ɪə	ear	here
eə	air	there
ʊə	poor	sure

/'/ 表示後面的音節須要重讀，如 today / təˈdeɪ /

Guide to the Dictionary 使用説明

詞目
合共510個，全屬基本詞彙。另有135個附加字詞列於書後，幫助理解例句。

解釋
只收最基本義，方便記憶。部分常用方言説法亦適當收錄。

讀音
詞目均以國際音標注明標準讀音。

插圖
全部詞目均圖文並茂，以幫助兒童理解詞義。

例句
中英對照；題材生活化，着重教授基本句式。

參考
翻到有關專題詞目，可增進更多知識。

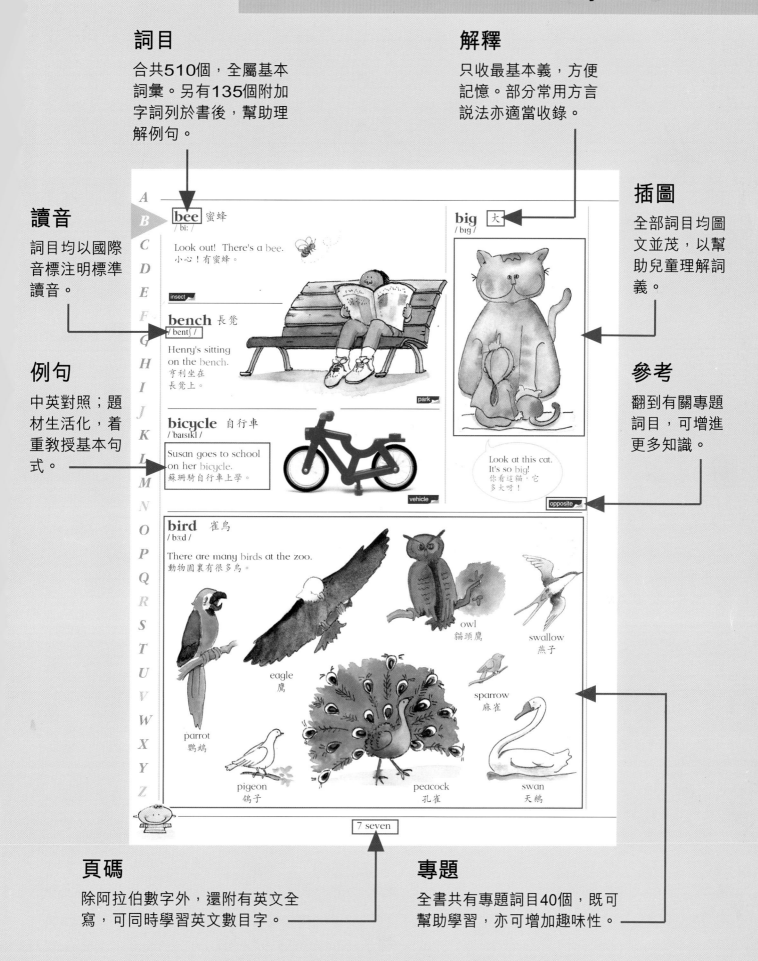

A B C D E F G H I J K L M N O P Q R S T U V W X Y Z

bee 蜜蜂
/ biː /
Look out! There's a bee.
小心！有蜜蜂。
insect

bench 長凳
/ bentʃ /
Henry's sitting on the bench.
亨利坐在長凳上。
park

bicycle 自行車
/ ˈbaɪsɪkl /
Susan goes to school on her bicycle.
蘇珊騎自行車上學。
vehicle

big 大
/ bɪg /
Look at this cat. It's so big!
你看這貓，它多大呀！
opposite

bird 雀鳥
/ bɜːd /
There are many birds at the zoo.
動物園裏有很多鳥。

owl 貓頭鷹
swallow 燕子
eagle 鷹
sparrow 麻雀
parrot 鸚鵡
pigeon 鴿子
peacock 孔雀
swan 天鵝

7 seven

頁碼
除阿拉伯數字外，還附有英文全寫，可同時學習英文數目字。

專題
全書共有專題詞目40個，既可幫助學習，亦可增加趣味性。

A α

actor 演員
/ ˈæktə /

Jack wants to be an actor.
杰克想當演員。

`job`

adult 成年人
/ ˈædʌlt /

Why should I listen to you ?
我為甚麼要聽你的話？
Because I'm an adult.
因為我是大人。

`people`

aeroplane 飛機
/ ˈeərəpleɪn /

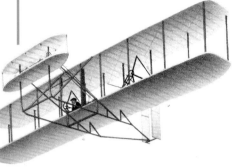

Wow, what an old aeroplane this is !
哇，這架飛機多古老！

afraid 害怕
/ əˈfreɪd /

What are you afraid of ?
你怕甚麼？

I'm afraid of you.
我怕你。

`feeling`

again 再次
/ əˈgen /

Try it again.
再試一次。

also 也；亦
/ ˈɔːlsəʊ /

I have a bicycle.
我有一輛自行車。

I also have one.
我也有一輛。

afternoon 下午
/ ˈɑːftəˈnuːn /

What are you going to do this afternoon ?
你今天下午打算做甚麼？
I'm going to play football.
我打算去踢足球。

`time`

always 總是；永遠
/ ˈɔːlweɪz /

Peter always goes to school by bus.
彼得總是坐公共汽車上學。

and 和；同
/ ənd /

Mary and I are good friends.
瑪麗和我是好朋友。

animal 動物
/ ˈænɪml /

Do you like animals?
你喜歡動物嗎？
No, I don't.
不，我不喜歡。

angry 生氣；憤怒
/ ˈæŋgrɪ /

Because you talk too much.
因為你說話太多。

Why are you angry with me?
你為甚麼生我的氣？

feeling

ant 螞蟻
/ ænt /

These are ants.
這些是螞蟻。

insect

apple 蘋果
/ ˈæpl /

Do you like apples?
你喜歡吃蘋果嗎？

fruit

a b c d e f g h i j k l m n o p q r s t u v w x y z

April 四月

/ˈeɪprəl /

When is April Fools' Day ?
愚人節是哪一天？
It's the first of April.
是四月一日。

month

Bb

arm 臂

/ ɑːm /

We are dancing arm in arm.
我們臂挽着臂跳舞。

body

baby 嬰兒

/ ˈbeɪbɪ /

What's the baby's name ?
這個嬰兒叫甚麼名字？
Her name is Yau Yau.
她叫悠悠。

people

August 八月

/ ˈɔːgəst /

There is no school in August.
八月份不用上學。
We can go swimming every day.
我們可以每天去游泳。

month

bad 差；壞

/ bæd /

What a bad day I had !
我今天真倒霉！

feeling

autumn 秋天

/ ˈɔːtəm /

The weather is always fine in autumn.
秋天天氣總是很好。

season

badminton 羽毛球
/ ˈbædmɪntn /

What are they doing ?
他們在做甚麼？
They're playing badminton.
他們在打羽毛球。

`sport`

ball 球
/ bɔːl /

Why don't you play tennis ?
你們為甚麼不打網球？
Because we haven't got a ball.
因為我們沒有球。

`toy`

balloon 氣球
/ bəˈluːn /

Give me a balloon !
給我一個氣球！
No, I won't.
我才不會。

`toy`

banana 香蕉
/ bəˈnɑːnə /

Monkeys like bananas.
猴子喜歡吃香蕉。

`fruit`

basketball 籃球
/ ˈbɑːskɪtbɔːl /

Is Peter good at basketball ?
彼得籃球打得好嗎？
Yes, he's very good at it.
對，他打得很好。

`sport`

bath 洗澡；浴缸
/ bɑːθ /

I'm taking a bath.
我在洗澡。

`bathroom`

bathroom 浴室
/ ˈbɑːθruːm /

Who's in the
bathroom ?
誰在浴室裏面？

It's me, Henry !
是我，亨利！

towel
毛巾

soap
肥皂

bath
浴缸

toilet
馬桶

toothpaste
牙膏

toothbrush
牙刷

mirror
鏡子

comb
梳子

home

beach 海灘
/ biːtʃ /

When will we go to the beach ?
我們甚麼時候去海灘？

Next Saturday.
下星期六。

place

bear 熊
/ beə /

I've never seen
a bear so big !
我從沒見過這麼
大的熊！

Neither
have I.
我也沒
見過。

zoo

beautiful 漂亮；美麗
/ ˈbjuːtɪfl /

Anne, you're so beautiful today !
安妮，你今天真漂亮！
Thank you.
謝謝。

opposite

because 因為
/ bɪˈkɒz /

Because she's angry with me.
因為她在生我的氣。

Jack, why don't you go out with Helen ?
杰克，你為甚麼不同海倫出去玩？

bed 床
/ bed /

Go to bed, Anne. It's late.
安妮，上床睡覺吧。
時間不早了。

bedroom

bedroom 寢室；睡房
/ ˈbedruːm /

Whose bedroom is this ?
這是誰的寢室？
It's my dad and mum's.
是我爸爸和媽媽的。

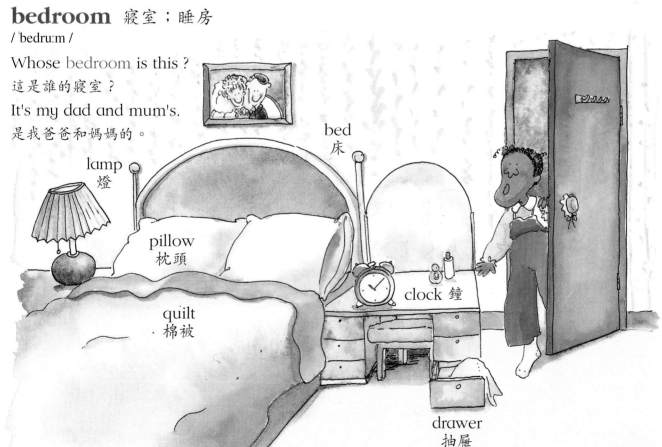

lamp 燈

bed 床

pillow 枕頭

quilt 棉被

clock 鐘

drawer 抽屜

home

bee 蜜蜂
/ bi: /

Look out！There's a bee.
小心！有蜜蜂。

`insect`

bench 長凳
/ bentʃ /

Henry's sitting on the bench.
亨利坐在長凳上。

`park`

bicycle 自行車
/ ˈbaɪsɪkl /

Susan goes to school on her bicycle.
蘇珊騎自行車上學。

`vehicle`

big 大
/ bɪg /

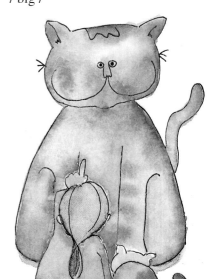

Look at this cat. It's so big！
你看這貓，它多大呀！

`opposite`

bird 雀鳥
/ bɜ:d /

There are many birds at the zoo.
動物園裏有很多鳥。

parrot
鸚鵡

eagle
鷹

pigeon
鴿子

peacock
孔雀

owl
貓頭鷹

swallow
燕子

sparrow
麻雀

swan
天鵝

birthday 生日
/ ˈbɜːθdeɪ /

Happy birthday !
生日快樂！
Thanks.
謝謝。

block 積木
/ blɒk /

David's building a house with blocks.
大衛在用積木蓋房子。 `toy`

blue 藍色
/ bluː /

How do you like my blue car ?
你覺得我這輛藍色汽車怎樣？

`colour`

biscuit 餅乾
/ ˈbɪskɪt /

Where's my biscuit ?
我的餅乾呢？

`food`

black 黑色
/ blæk /

I'm a woman in black.
我是個黑衣婦。

`colour`

blackboard 黑板
/ ˈblækbɔːd /

Amy has a small blackboard.
艾美有一個小黑板。 `classroom`

body 身體；軀幹
/ ˈbɒdɪ /

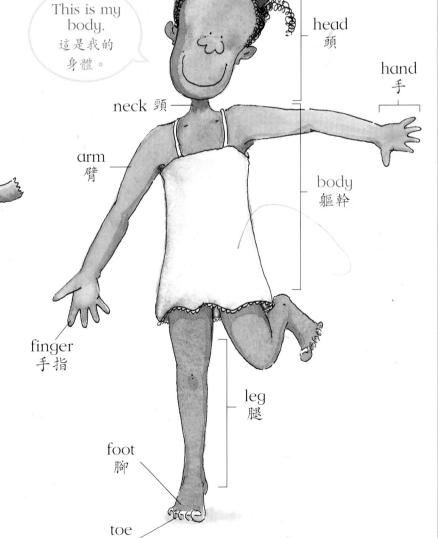

This is my body.
這是我的身體。

head 頭
hand 手
neck 頸
arm 臂
body 軀幹
finger 手指
leg 腿
foot 腳
toe 腳趾

a b c d e f g h i j k l m n o p q r s t u v w x y z

book 書
/ bʊk /

Is this the book you want ?
這是你要的書嗎？
Yes, it is.
對，就是這本。

`classroom`

bottle 瓶子
/ ˈbɒtl /

Look, he's
playing
with bottles !
看，他在耍瓶子！

`dining-room`

bowl 碗
/ bəʊl /

Is this bowl yours ?
這是你的碗嗎？
Yes, it is.
對，是我的。

`dining-room`

box 箱子；盒子
/ bɒks /

Do you have a
jack-in-the-box ?
你有玩偶盒嗎？

boy 男孩
/ bɔɪ /

What's this boy's name ?
這個男孩叫甚麼名字？
His name is John.
他叫約翰。

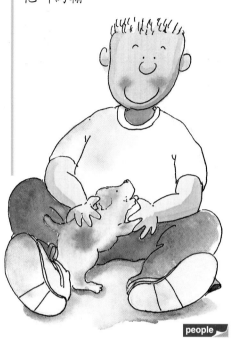

`people`

bread 麵包
/ bred /

I like bread
very much.
我很喜歡吃
麵包。

`food`

breakfast 早餐
/ ˈbrekfəst /

Julie has breakfast at
seven o'clock.
朱莉七點鐘吃早餐。

brother 兄弟

/ ˈbrʌðə /

How many brothers does Mary have ?

瑪麗有多少個兄弟？

She has two. They're Paul and Jack.

她有兩個。他們是保羅和杰克。

`family`

butterfly 蝴蝶

/ ˈbʌtəflaɪ /

Look at these butterflies. How beautiful they are !

你看這些蝴蝶。它們多漂亮啊！

`insect`

brown 棕色；咖啡色

/ braʊn /

All of these are brown.

這些都是咖啡色的。

`colour`

bus 公共汽車；巴士(方言)

/ bʌs /

Go to school by bus if you don't want to be late.

你如果不想遲到，就坐公共汽車上學。

`vehicle`

bye-bye 再見

/ baɪˈbaɪ /

Don't be late tomorrow. Bye-bye !

明天不要遲到。再見！

butter 黃油；牛油(方言)

/ ˈbʌtə /

John eats a lot of butter.

約翰吃很多黃油。

That's why he's so fat.

所以他這麼胖。

`food`

a b c d e f g h i j k l m n o p q r s t u v w x y z

Cc

cake 蛋糕
/ keɪk /

Wow, whose birthday cake is this ?

哇，這是誰的生日蛋糕？

It's Susan's.

是蘇珊的。

`food`

can 能夠；會
/ kæn /

Can you stand on one arm ?

你能夠單臂倒立嗎？

Yes, I can.
我能夠。

car 汽車
/ ka: /

This is the best car of the year.

這是本年度最佳汽車。

`vehicle`

card 紙牌
/ ka:d /

John likes playing cards very much.

約翰很喜歡玩紙牌。 `toy`

carrot 胡蘿蔔
/ ˈkærət /

I like carrots very very much.
我非常非常喜歡吃胡蘿蔔。

`vegetable`

cat 貓
/ kæt /

Anne's afraid of cats.

安妮怕貓。

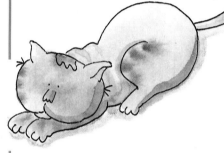

Why ? She's not a mouse !

為甚麼？她又不是老鼠！

chair 椅子
/ tʃeə /

Amy is sitting on the chair reading.

艾美坐在椅子上看書。

`classroom`
`dining-room`

chalk 粉筆
/ tʃɒk /

The teacher uses chalk to write on the blackboard.
老師用粉筆在黑板上寫字。

`classroom`

chess 棋
/ tʃes /

What are Mary and Julie doing？
瑪麗和朱莉在做甚麼？
They're playing chess.
她們在下棋。

`toy`

chicken 雞
/ ˈtʃɪkɪn /

Would you like to have chicken for dinner？
晚餐你想吃雞嗎？

`farm`

child 兒童
/ tʃaɪld /

Who's the child sleeping on the sofa？
睡在沙發上的小孩是誰？

`people`

chopsticks 筷子
/ ˈtʃɒpstɪks /

The Chinese eat with chopsticks.
中國人用筷子吃飯。

`dining-room`

cinema 電影院
/ ˈsɪnəmə /

Where did you go last night？
你昨晚去了哪兒？
I went to the cinema.
我去了看電影。

`place`

chocolate 巧克力
/ ˈtʃɒklət /

Do you want some chocolate？
吃巧克力嗎？
No, thanks.
不，謝謝。

`food`

circle 圓形
/ ˈsɜːkl /

These are circles.
這些是圓形。

`shape`

classroom 課室

/ˈklɑːsruːm /

This is our classroom.
這是我們的課室。

blackboard
黑板

chalk 粉筆

book
書

teacher
教師

desk
書桌

pupil 學生

chair 椅子

ruler 尺

paper 紙

pencil 鉛筆

pen 原子筆

rubber 橡皮擦

clean 乾淨

/ kliːn /

This toilet is very clean.

這個馬桶很乾淨。

`opposite`

clock 鐘

/ klɒk /

What time is it, Mary?

瑪麗，現在幾點鐘？

Why don't
you look at the clock?

你為甚麼不看一看鐘？

`bedroom`

close 關閉

/ kləʊz /

Close the window, Amy.
It's raining.

艾美，把窗關上，下雨了。

clothes 衣服

/ kləʊðz /

Do you like my clothes?
你喜歡我的衣服嗎？

No, I don't.
不，我不喜歡。

hat 帽子

coat 外套

shirt 襯衣

shorts 短褲

trousers 褲子

sock 襪子

dress 裙子

shoe 鞋子

cloud 雲
/ klaʊd /

Look at that cloud.
你看那片雲。
Wow, it looks like a sheep !
哇，它看起來很像一隻羊！

weather

coat 外套
/ kəʊt /

Put on your coat, Henry. It's cold.
亨利，穿上你的外套吧，天氣很冷。

clothes

coconut 椰子
/ ˈkəʊkənʌt /

What's this ?
這是甚麼？
This is a coconut.
這是椰子。

fruit

cold 冷
/ kəʊld /

My God, it's very cold today !
天啊，今天冷得要命！

opposite

colour 顏色
/ ˈkʌlə /

What colour is this ?
這是甚麼顏色？

red 紅色

orange 橙色

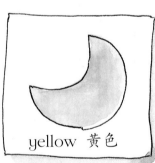
yellow 黃色

green 綠色

blue 藍色

purple 紫色

pink 粉紅色

brown 咖啡色

black 黑色

grey 灰色

white 白色

15 fifteen

comb 梳子
/ kəʊm /

Do you have a comb?
你有梳子嗎？

Sorry, I don't.
對不起，
我沒有。

bathroom

cow 牛；母牛
/ kaʊ /

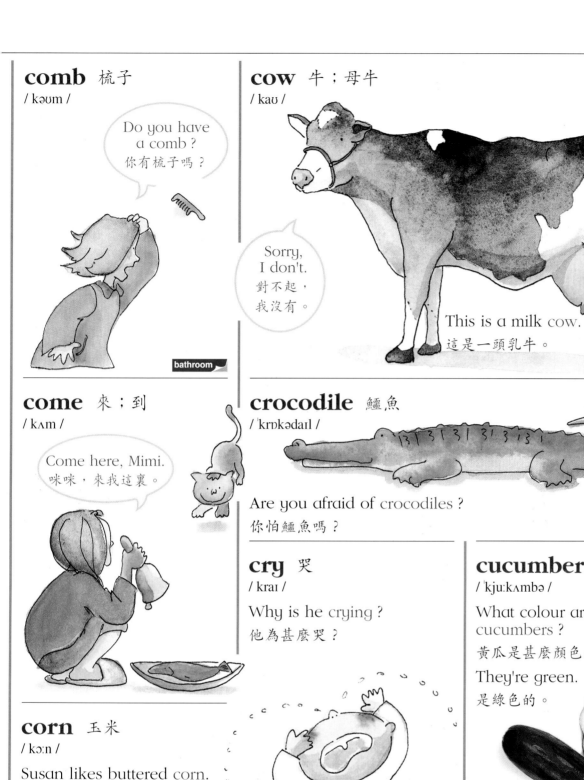

This is a milk cow.
這是一頭乳牛。

farm

come 來；到
/ kʌm /

Come here, Mimi.
咪咪，來我這裏。

crocodile 鱷魚
/ ˈkrɒkədaɪl /

Are you afraid of crocodiles?
你怕鱷魚嗎？

zoo

corn 玉米
/ kɔːn /

Susan likes buttered corn.
蘇珊喜歡吃黃油玉米。

vegetable

cry 哭
/ kraɪ /

Why is he crying?
他為甚麼哭？

Because he's hungry.
因為他肚子餓。

people

cucumber 黃瓜；青瓜
/ ˈkjuːkʌmbə /

What colour are cucumbers?
黃瓜是甚麼顏色的？

They're green.
是綠色的。

vegetable

cup 杯
/ kʌp /

Would you like a cup of tea?
你想來一杯茶嗎？

sitting-room

a b c d e f g h i j k l m n o p q r s t u v w x y z

cupboard 碗櫥
/ ˈkʌbəd /

There are many bowls and plates in the cupboard.
碗櫥裏有很多碗碟。

`kitchen`

Dd

dance 跳舞
/ dɑːns /

She dances very well.
她跳舞跳得很好。

daughter 女兒
/ ˈdɔːtə /

This is my daughter Anne.
這是我女兒安妮。

`family`

cycling 騎自行車
/ ˈsaɪklɪŋ /

Henry often goes cycling with Anne on Saturdays.
亨利星期六經常同安妮去騎自行車。

`sport`

day 一天；白天
/ deɪ /

There are twenty-four hours in a day.
一天有二十四小時。

December 十二月
/ dɪˈsembə /

Christmas Day is on the twenty-fifth of December.
聖誕節是十二月二十五日。

`month`

department store 百貨公司

/ dɪˈpɑːtmənt stɔː /

Hong Kong has many big department stores.

香港有很多大百貨公司。

place

desk 書桌

/ desk /

Whose desk is this?

這是誰的桌子？

This is John's desk.

這是約翰的桌子。

classroom

dining-room 飯廳

/ ˈdaɪnɪŋruːm /

This is our dining-room.

這是我們的飯廳。

bottle 瓶子

chair 椅子

chopsticks 筷子

plate 盤子

spoon 匙

fork 叉子

bowl 碗

dinner 晚餐

/ ˈdɪnə /

We have dinner at eight.

我們八點鐘吃晚飯。

home

knife 刀

glass 玻璃杯

table 桌子

dirty 骯髒
/ ˈdɜːtɪ /

Your face is very dirty. Go and wash it now.

你的臉很髒，快去洗臉。

`opposite`

dog 狗
/ dɒg /

John's grandpa has a dog.

約翰的爺爺養了一隻狗。

down 往下
/ daʊn /

Henry jumped down from the tree.

亨利從樹上跳了下來。 `where`

do 做
/ duː /

What's Paul doing?

保羅在做甚麼？

He's doing his homework.

他在做家庭作業。

doll 洋娃娃
/ dɒl /

Mary's looking for her doll.

瑪麗在找她的洋娃娃。

`toy`

dragonfly 蜻蜓
/ ˈdrægənflaɪ /

Anne's drawing a dragonfly.

安妮在畫蜻蜓。

doctor 醫生
/ ˈdɒktə /

What's wrong with me, Doctor?
醫生，我怎麼啦？

`job`

door 門
/ dɔː /

Amy opened the door.

艾美把門開了。 `sitting-room`

draw 繪畫
/ drɔː /

`insect`

What's Anne drawing?

安妮在畫甚麼？

drawer 抽屜
/ drɔː /

Where are my socks ?
我的襪子在哪兒？

They're in the second drawer.
在第二個抽屜裏面。

bedroom

dress 裙子
/ dres /

Your dress is very beautiful.
你的裙子很漂亮。

Thank you.
謝謝。

clothes

drink 喝
/ drɪŋk /

Mary's drinking orange juice.
瑪麗在喝橙汁。

driver 司機
/ ˈdraɪvə /

John's father is a bus-driver.
約翰的父親是公共汽車司機。

job

drum 鼓
/ drʌm /

Whose drum is this ?
這是誰的鼓？

It's Paul's.
是保羅的。

music

duck 鴨子
/ dʌk /

There are five ducks
一共有五隻鴨子。

farm

Ee

eagle 鷹
/ ˈiːgl /

Sometimes we can see eagles making circles in the sky.
有時我們可以看到鷹在天空打轉。
bird

ear 耳朵
/ ɪə /

Rabbits have long ears.
兔子的耳朵很長。

face

early 早
/ ˈɜːlɪ /

Susan gets up early in the morning.
蘇珊早上很早起床。

opposite

a b c d e f g h i j k l m n o p q r s t u v w x y z

eat 吃
/ iːt /

John's eating all the time.

約翰吃個沒停。

egg 雞蛋
/ eg /

Eggs are good for you.

雞蛋對你有好處。 food

eight 八
/ eɪt /

Four and four are eight.

四加四等於八。 number

eighteen 十八
/ eɪˈtiːn /

Two nines are eighteen.

二乘九等於十八。

number

eighty 八十
/ ˈeɪtɪ /

Pay eighty dollars and I'll be yours.

付八十塊錢，那我就是你的。

$80. number

elephant 象
/ ˈelɪfənt /

David saw an elephant at the zoo yesterday.

大衛昨天在動物園看見大象。

zoo

eleven 十一
/ ɪˈlevn /

There are two ones in eleven.

十一裏面有兩個一。 number

English 英語
/ ˈɪŋglɪʃ /

Can you speak English ?
你會講英語嗎？

Yes, I can.
對，我會。

evening
/ ˈiːvnɪŋ /

晚間(下午六時至睡覺前)

Julie was at home watching television yesterday evening.

朱莉昨晚在家裏看電視。 time

eye 眼睛
/ aɪ /

We see with our eyes.

我們用眼睛來看。

face

Ff

fable 寓言
/ ˈfeɪbl /

Do you know this fable ?
你知道這個寓言嗎？

face 臉；面孔
/ feɪs /

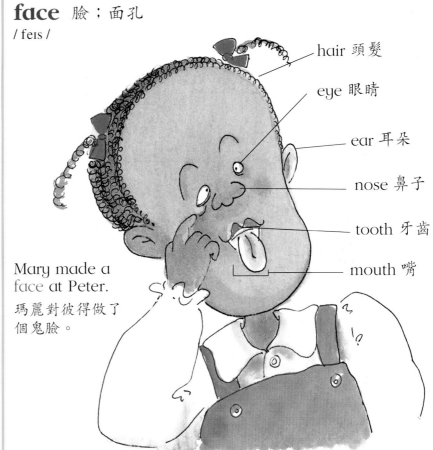

hair 頭髮

eye 眼睛

ear 耳朵

nose 鼻子

tooth 牙齒

mouth 嘴

Mary made a face at Peter.
瑪麗對彼得做了個鬼臉。

family 家庭；家人
/ ˈfæməlɪ /

I have a happy family.
我有一個快樂的家庭。

sister 姊妹

daughter 女兒

brother 兄弟

son 兒子

mother 媽媽

father 爸爸

grandfather 祖父

grandmother 祖母

fan 扇；電風扇
/ fæn /

This fan is wonderful !
這風扇真棒！

sitting-room

farm 農場
/ fɑːm /

Amy's father has a very big farm.
艾美的父親有一個很大的農場。

sheep 羊

horse 馬

farmer 農夫

cow 牛

pig 豬

chicken 雞

duck 鴨子

goose 鵝

job

farmer 農夫
/ ˈfɑːmə /

Amy's father is a farmer.
艾美的父親是個農夫。

place

fast 快
/ fɑːst /

This is the fastest car in the world.
這是全世界最快的汽車。

opposite

fat 胖
/ fæt /

John is so fat !
約翰多麼胖！

opposite

father 父親；爸爸
/ ˈfɑ:ðə /

This is my father.
這是我父親。

family

February 二月
/ ˈfebruərɪ /

Saint Valentine's Day is on the fourteenth of February.
情人節是二月十四日。

February 2

S日	M一	T二	W三	T四	F五	S六
				1	2	3	4
5	6	7	8	9	10	11
12	13	14	15	16	17	18
19	20	21	22	23	24	25
26	27	28				

month

feeling 感覺；預感
/ ˈfi:lɪŋ /

Do you have these feelings ?
你有這些感覺嗎？

angry 生氣

afraid 害怕

sad 悲傷

happy 快樂

ill 生病

well 健康

sorry 抱歉

thirsty 口渴

hungry 飢餓

tired 疲倦

fifteen 十五
/ fɪfˈtiːn /

Three fives are fifteen.

三乘五等於十五。

number

finger 手指
/ ˈfɪŋgə /

Can you do this with your fingers ?

你可以用手指做這個嗎？

body

fifty 五十
/ ˈfɪftɪ /

How much do you have ?

你有多少錢？

I have fifty dollars.

我有五十塊錢。

$50=

number

fire 火
/ ˈfaɪə /

The house is on fire !

房子着火了！

fine 美好；晴朗
/ faɪn /

We go cycling today because the weather is fine.

今天天氣好，所以我們去騎自行車。

fireman 消防員
/ ˈfaɪəmən /

Julie wants to be a fireman.

朱莉想當消防員。

job

fire station 消防局
/ ˈfaɪə steɪʃn /

What's this ?

這是甚麼？

This is a fire station.

這是消防局。

place

A B C D E F G H I J K L M N O P Q R S T U V W X Y Z

first 第一；首先
/ fɜːst /

Henry came first in the race.

亨利賽跑得了第一。

`where`

fish 魚
/ fɪʃ /

Fish can swim.

魚會游泳。

five 五
/ faɪv /

This taxi can take five people.

這輛的士能夠載五個人。

`number`

flat 住宅單位
/ flæt /

How many bedrooms does this flat have ?

這個住宅單位有多少個睡房？

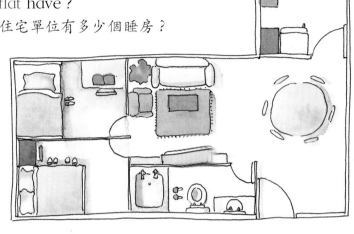

`home`

floor 地板
/ flɔː /

Mother cleans the floor every morning.

媽媽每天早上都打掃地板。

`sitting-room`

flower 花
/ ˈflaʊə /

What a beautiful flower !

多麼漂亮的花兒！

`park`

fly 飛；蒼蠅
/ flaɪ /

What are you doing ?
你在做甚麼？

I'm flying.
我在飛。

`insect`

a b c d e f g h i j k l m n o p q r s t u v w x y z

food 食物；食品

/ fuːd /

What food is this ?

這是甚麼食物 ?

chocolate
巧克力

sweets
糖果

milk
牛奶

jam
果醬

biscuits
餅乾

juice
果汁

butter
黃油

ice-cream
冰淇淋

bread
麵包

eggs
雞蛋

cake
蛋糕

rice
米飯

sausages
香腸

meat
肉

noodles
麵條

soup
湯

foot 腳

/ fʊt /

Can you stand on one foot ?
你能夠單腳站立嗎？

No, but I can stand on two feet.
不能，但我能夠雙腳站立。

`body`

four 四

/ fɔː /

A chair has four legs.
一張椅子有四條腿。

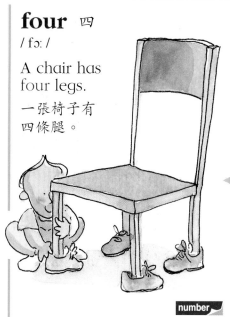

`number`

football 足球

/ ˈfʊtbɔːl /

What are Paul and Peter doing ?
保羅和彼得在做甚麼？

They're playing football.
他們在踢足球。

`sport`

fourteen 十四

/ fɔːˈtiːn /

Ten and four make fourteen.
十加四等於十四。

$$+$$

14

`number`

fork 叉子

/ fɔːk /

John likes eating with two forks.
約翰喜歡用兩個叉子吃東西。

`dining-room`

forty 四十

/ ˈfɔːtɪ /

Susan's mother is forty years old.
蘇珊的母親今年四十歲。

`number`

Friday 星期五

/ ˈfraɪdɪ /

Today is Black Friday.
今天是黑色星期五。

13 FRIDAY

`week`

fridge 冰箱；雪櫃(方言)

/ frɪdʒ /

Where's the ice-cream ?

冰淇淋在哪兒？

It's in the fridge.

在冰箱裏。

kitchen

friend 朋友

/ frend /

Julie has made a lot of friends at the park.

朱莉在公園裏交了很多朋友。

fruit 水果

/ fruːt /

Which of these fruits do you like ?

你喜歡吃哪種水果？

oranges
橙

apples
蘋果

pineapple
菠蘿

bananas
香蕉

grapes
葡萄

lemons
檸檬

coconuts
椰子

watermelons
西瓜

Gg

get 得到；變得
/ get /

Mary got a crocodile for her birthday.

瑪麗得到一條鱷魚作為生日禮物。

get off
下車

get up
起床

get on
上車

give 給；送
/ gɪv /

Father Christmas gave Susan a sweet.

聖誕老人送給蘇珊一塊糖果。

opposite

glass 玻璃杯
/ glɑːs /

Please give me a glass of water.

請給我一杯水。

sitting-room

good 好；乖
/ gud /

Henry is a good boy.

亨利是個乖孩子。

opposite

girl 女孩
/ gɜːl /

Who's that girl ?

那個女孩是誰？

She's my friend Anne.

她是我的朋友安妮。

family

go 去
/ gəʊ /

I must go to the library now.
我現在必須去圖書館。

OK, see you tomorrow.
好吧，明天見。

opposite

goose 鵝
/ guːs /

There's a goose over here.

這裏有一隻鵝。

No, there are two geese.

不，有兩隻鵝才對。

farm

grandfather
/ ˈgrænfɑːðə /

祖父；外祖父

Grandfather likes reading very much.

祖父很喜歡閱讀。

grandmother
/ ˈgrænmʌðə /

祖母；外祖母

Grandmother made me a new pullover.

祖母給我做了一件新毛衣。

grey 灰色
/ greɪ /

Look at those grey clouds. It's going to rain.

瞧那些灰雲，快下雨了。

`colour`

`family`

grape 葡萄
/ greɪp /

Where did you get those grapes ?

你那些葡萄是在哪兒買的？

At the supermarket.

在超級市場。

`fruit`

guitar 吉他
/ gɪˈtɑː /

You play the guitar very well.
你的吉他彈得很好。

Thank you.
謝謝。

grass 草
/ grɑːs /

Grass is food for many animals.

草是很多動物的食物。

green 綠色
/ griːn /

All of these are green.

這些都是綠色的。

`park`　　　`colour`

`music`

Hh

hair 頭髮
/ heə /

Your hair is very beautiful.
你的頭髮很漂亮。

Thank you.
謝謝。

face

hand 手
/ hænd /

Whose hand is this?
這是誰的手？

body

happy 快樂；高興
/ ˈhæpɪ /

Why are you so happy?
你為甚麼這樣高興？

I've got a new car.
我得到一輛新汽車。

feeling   opposite

harmonica 口琴
/ hɑːˈmɒnɪkə /

Can you play the harmonica?
你會吹口琴嗎？

No, I can't.
不，我不會。

music

he 他
/ hiː /

Who is he?
他是誰？

He's my friend Henry.
他是我的朋友亨利。

head 頭
/ hed /

What's on my head?
我頭上有甚麼？

A butterfly.
一隻蝴蝶。

body

hat 帽子
/ hæt /

This is my favourite hat.
這是我最喜愛的帽子。

clothes

hear 聽見
/ hɪə /

Do you hear me?
你聽見我說的話嗎？

Yes, I do.
對，我聽見。

a b c d e f g h i j k l m n o p q r s t u v w x y z

hello 喂；你好
/ həˈləʊ /

Hello, Peter.
彼得，你好。

Hello, Amy.
艾美，你好。

her 她；她的
/ hɜ: /

Where's Susan ?
蘇珊在哪兒？

She's in her bedroom.
她在她房間裏面。

here 這裏
/ hɪə /

Where are you, Mimi ?
咪咪，你在哪兒？

I'm here.
我在這裏。

high 高
/ haɪ /

The grapes are too high. David can't get them.
葡萄太高了，大衛摘不到。

opposite

him 他
/ hɪm /

Don't talk to him.
不要跟他說話。

Why ? He's my friend.
為甚麼？他是我的朋友。

his 他的
/ hɪz /

What's Paul doing ?
保羅在做甚麼？
He's washing his dog.
他在替他的狗洗澡。

home 家
/ həʊm /

My home is Hong Kong.
香港是我家。

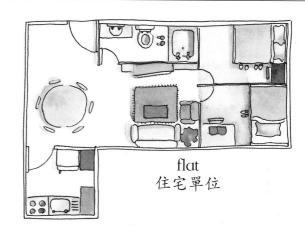
flat
住宅單位

house
房子

bedroom
睡房

dining-room
飯廳

bathroom
浴室

sitting-room
客廳

kitchen
廚房

a b c d e f g **h** i j k l m n o p q r s t u v w x y z

horse 馬
/ hɔːs /

What's Julie doing ?
朱莉在做甚麼？
She's riding a horse.
她在騎馬。

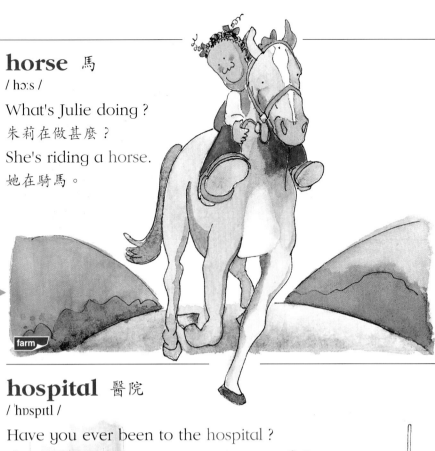

farm

hospital 醫院
/ ˈhɒspɪtl /

Have you ever been to the hospital ?
你去過醫院嗎？
Yes, I have.
我去過。

place

hot 熱
/ hɒt /

It's very hot in summer.
夏天天氣很熱。

opposite

hour 小時
/ ˈaʊə /

How many hours do you sleep a day ?
你一天睡多少個小時？
I sleep eight hours a day.
我一天睡八個小時。

house 房子；房屋
/ haʊs /

What a big house this is !
這所房子真大！

home

how 怎樣
/ haʊ /

How can I get the mouse ?
我怎樣可以捉到老鼠？

hundred 一百
/ ˈhʌndred /

One hundred pounds !
You're too heavy.

一百磅！你太重了。

100 ?!

number

hungry 飢餓
/ ˈhʌŋgrɪ /

Why are you so hungry ?

你為甚麼這麼餓？

I didn't have breakfast this morning.

我今天早上沒吃早餐。

feeling

I i

I 我
/ aɪ /

Jack and I are brothers.

杰克和我是兄弟。

ice-cream
/ aɪsˈkriːm /

冰淇淋；雪糕(方言)

Ice-cream is my favourite food.

冰淇淋是我最喜愛的食物。

food

if 如果
/ ɪf /

If I could fly...

如果我能夠飛...

ill 生病
/ ɪl /

Anne is ill.

安妮病了。

She must go to see a doctor.

她必須去看醫生。

feeling

in 在家；在...裏面
/ ɪn /

Hello, is Peter in ?

喂，彼得在家嗎？

where

a b c d e f g h i j k l m n o p q r s t u v w x y z

Jj

insect 昆蟲
/ ˈɪnsekt /

An insect has six legs.
昆蟲有六隻腳。

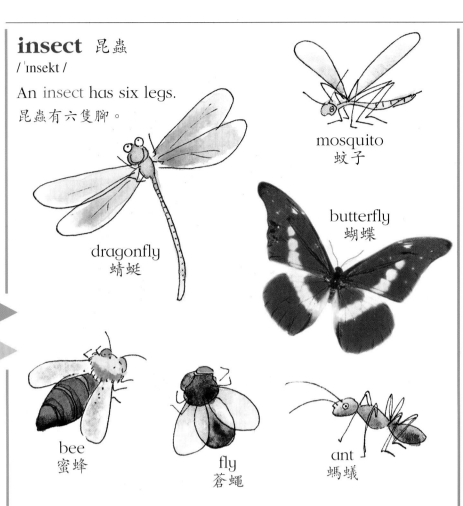

mosquito
蚊子

butterfly
蝴蝶

dragonfly
蜻蜓

bee
蜜蜂

fly
蒼蠅

ant
螞蟻

jam 果醬
/ dʒæm /

What jam does Amy like ?
艾美喜歡甚麼果醬？
She likes strawberry jam.
她喜歡草莓果醬。

food

it 它
/ ɪt /

Where should I put the vase ?
我應該把花瓶放在哪兒？
Put it on the table.
把它放在桌子上。

its 它的
/ ɪts /

This is my cat.
Its name is Mimi.
這是我的貓，它的
名字叫咪咪。

January 一月
/ ˈdʒænjʊərɪ /

It is very cold in January.
一月份天氣很冷。

January 1
S日 M一 T二 W三 T四 F五 S六
1 2 3 4 5 6 7
8 9 10 11 12 13 14
15 16 17 18 19 20 21
22 23 24 25 26 27 28
29 30 31

month

job 職業
/ dʒɒb /

What is your job ?
你的職業是甚麼 ?

actor
演員

singer
歌手

teacher
老師

doctor
醫生

postman
郵差

fireman
消防員

nurse
護士

farmer
農夫

policeman
警察

driver
司機

a b c d e f g h i j k l m n o p q r s t u v w x y z

juice 果汁
/ dʒuːs /

What juice does Susan like ?
蘇珊喜歡喝甚麼果汁？
She likes apple juice.
她喜歡喝蘋果汁。

food

Kk

July 七月
/ dʒuːˈlaɪ /

It is very hot in July.
七月份天氣很熱。

month

June 六月
/ dʒuːn /

When is David's birthday ?
大衛的生日是甚麼時候？
It's the tenth of June.
是六月十日。

month

kangaroo 袋鼠
/ kæŋɡəˈruː /

There are many kangaroos in Australia.
澳洲有很多袋鼠。

zoo

jump 跳
/ dʒʌmp /

Susan, why did you jump on the chair ?
蘇珊，你為甚麼跳到椅子上？

Because there's a mouse on the floor.
因為地上有老鼠。

just 剛剛
/ dʒʌst /

The train has just gone.
火車剛開了。

key 鑰匙
/ kiː /

This is a key.
這是鑰匙。

kick 踢
/ kɪk /

Paul kicked the ball.
保羅把球踢出去了。

kind 仁慈；和藹
/ kaɪnd /

Julie is always very kind.
朱莉總是很仁慈。

kiss 吻
/ kɪs /

You see, mothers always kiss their babies.
你看，母親總愛吻
她們的寶貝。

kitchen 廚房
/ ˈkɪtʃɪn /

Where's Julie?
朱莉在哪兒？
She's in the kitchen.
她在廚房裏面。

cupboard
碗櫥

fridge
冰箱

tap
水龍頭

sink
洗滌槽

stove
爐子

oven
烤爐

knife 刀
/ naɪf /

I'll cut the oranges with this knife.
我會用這把刀切橙。

dining-room

home

a b c d e f g h i j k l m n o p q r s t u v w x y z

Ll

laugh 笑
/ lɑ:f /

What are you laughing at ?
你在笑甚麼？

Your picture.
你的照片。

lamp 燈
/ læmp /

Turn on the lamp, please.
請把燈開了。

bedroom

left 左
/ left /

The driver put up his left hand.
司機舉起了他的左手。

opposite

last 最後；上一個
/ lɑ:st /

I'm the last one.
我是最後一個。

where

leg 腿
/ leg /

Helen has long legs.
海倫有修長的腿。

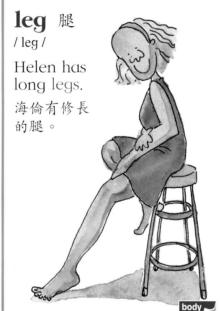

body

lemon 檸檬
/ ˈlemən /

What's this ?
這是甚麼？

This is a lemon.
這是檸檬。

fruit

lettuce
/ ˈletɪs /
萵苣；生菜

Peter doesn't like lettuce.
彼得不喜歡吃生菜。

vegetable

late 遲；晚
/ leɪt /

Oh !
I'm late.
啊！我來晚了。

opposite

library 圖書館
/ ˈlaɪbrərɪ /

There are many books in the library.
圖書館有很多書。

place

like 喜歡；和...一樣
/ laɪk /

Julie's hat is like Anne's.
朱莉的帽子和安妮的一樣。

lock 鎖
/ lɒk /

We open a lock with a key.
我們用鑰匙開鎖。

long 長
/ lɒŋ /

Your hair is very long.
你的頭髮很長。

opposite

lion 獅子
/ ˈlaɪən /

David saw a lion at the zoo yesterday.
大衛昨天在動物園看見獅子。

ZOO

look 看
/ lʊk /

Henry is looking at the clock.
亨利在看鐘。

look for
尋找

look out
小心

listen 聽
/ ˈlɪsn /

What's Amy doing ?
艾美在做甚麼？

She's listening to music.
她在聽音樂。

lorry 貨車
/ ˈlɒrɪ /

Whose lorry is this ?
這是誰的貨車？

It's my father's.
是我父親的。

vehicle

a b c d e f g h i j k l m n o p q r s t u v w x y z

low 低；矮
/ ləʊ /

This table is very low.
這張桌子很矮。

opposite

Mm

make 製造；做
/ meɪk /

Julie is making a cake.
朱莉在做蛋糕。

man 男人
/ mæn /

There's a man over there.
那邊有一個男人。
No, there are two men.
不，有兩個男人才對。

people

lunch 午餐
/ lʌntʃ /

What's Peter doing ?
彼得在做甚麼？
He's having his lunch.
他在吃午飯。

March 三月
/ mɑːtʃ /

John will be nine years old next March.
約翰明年三月就九歲了。

month

market 市場
/ ˈmɑːkɪt /

Where are we ?
我們在哪兒？
We're at the market.
我們在市場。

place

May 五月
/ meɪ /
When is Anne's birthday?
安妮的生日是甚麼時候？
It's the fourth of May.
是五月四日。

`month`

may 可以
/ meɪ /

May I come in?
我可以進來嗎？

me 我
/ miː /

Give me the book.
把書給我。

No, I won't.
我才不會。

meat 肉
/ miːt /
What meat do you like?
你喜歡吃甚麼肉？
I like pork and beef.
我喜歡吃豬肉和牛肉。

`food`

milk 牛奶
/ mɪlk /
Give me a glass of milk, please.
請給我一杯牛奶。

`food`

mirror 鏡子
/ ˈmɪrə /
How many horses are there in the mirror?
鏡子裏面有多少匹馬？

There are four.
有四匹馬。
`bathroom`

Monday 星期一
/ ˈmʌndɪ /
I'll go to the library on Monday.
我星期一會去圖書館。

`week`

monkey 猴子
/ ˈmʌŋkɪ /

How many monkeys are there?
一共有多少隻猴子？
There are four.
一共有四隻。
`zoo`

a b c d e f g h i j k l m n o p q r s t u v w x y z

month 月；月份
/ mʌnθ /

There are twelve months in a year.
一年有十二個月。

January 一月

February 二月

March 三月

April 四月

May 五月

June 六月

July 七月

August 八月

September 九月

October 十月

November 十一月

December 十二月

moon 月亮
/ muːn /

The moon is very beautiful tonight !
今晚的月亮很美麗！

mosquito 蚊子
/ məsˈkiːtəʊ /

A mosquito is an insect.
蚊子是一種昆蟲。

insect

morning 早上
/ ˈmɔːnɪŋ /

Grandpa and Grandma go for a walk every morning.
爺爺奶奶每天早上都去散步。

when

mother 母親；媽媽
/ ˈmʌðə /

This is my mother.
Is she beautiful ?
這是我媽媽，她漂亮嗎？

family

motorbike 摩托車

/ ˈməʊtəbaɪk /

A policeman is riding a motorbike

警察在騎摩托車。

vehicle ▶

mouse 老鼠

/ maʊs /

There's a mouse over there.

那裏有一隻老鼠。

No, there are two mice.

不，有兩隻老鼠才對。

mouth 嘴；口

/ maʊθ /

I have a big mouth.

我的嘴很大。

face ▶

mushroom 蘑菇

/ ˈmʌʃrʊm /

Amy likes mushroom soup.

艾美喜歡喝蘑菇湯。

vegetable ▶

music 音樂

/ ˈmjuːzɪk /

Do you like music ?

你喜歡音樂嗎？

Yes, very much.

是的，很喜歡。

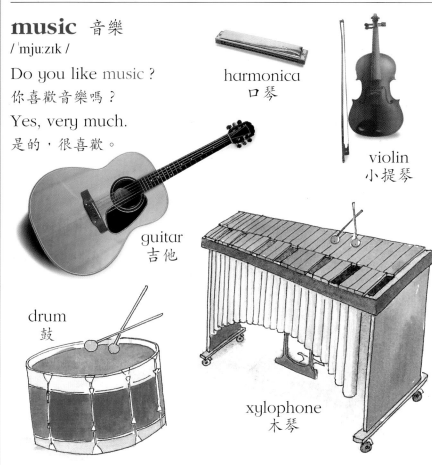

harmonica 口琴

violin 小提琴

guitar 吉他

drum 鼓

xylophone 木琴

piano 鋼琴

a b c d e f g h i j k l m n o p q r s t u v w x y z

must 必須
/ mʌst /

You must wash your hands first.
你必須先洗手。

Yes, Mother.
是的，媽媽。

my 我的
/ maɪ /

This is my picture.
這是我的照片。

Nn

name 名字；名稱
/ neɪm /

My name is David.
我的名字叫大衛。

neck 頸；脖子
/ nek /

A giraffe has a very long neck.
長頸鹿的脖子很長。

body

never 從不
/ ˈnevə /

Anne never likes fish.
安妮從不喜歡吃魚。

new 新
/ njuː /

Are these shoes new ?
這雙鞋是新的嗎？

Yes, they are.
對，是新的。

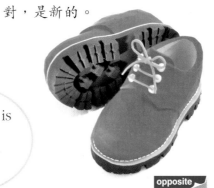

opposite

next 下一個
/ nekst /

Nobody wants to be the next.
沒有人想做下一個。

Next !
下一個！

night 晚上
/ naɪt /

What do you do at night ?
你晚上做甚麼？

I read.
我閱讀。

time

nine 九

/ naɪn /

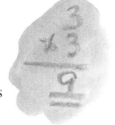

Three threes are nine.

三乘三等於九。

`number`

nineteen 十九

/ naɪnˈtiːn /

Helen is nineteen years old.

海倫今年十九歲。

`number`

ninety 九十

/ ˈnaɪntɪ /

This building has ninety storeys.

這座大樓有九十層。

`number`

noodle 麵條

/ ˈnuːdl /

Paul likes noodles for breakfast.

保羅早餐喜歡吃麵條。

`food`

noon 中午

/ nuːn /

What time is it?
現在是甚麼時候?

It's noon.
現在是中午。

`time`

nose 鼻子

/ nəʊz /

Peter has a big nose.

彼得的鼻子很大。

`face`

November 十一月

/ nəˈvembə /

Whose birthday is the second of November?
十一月二日是誰的生日?

November 11

It's Amy's birthday.
是艾美的生日。

`month`

now 現在

/ naʊ /

Where are you going now?
你現在去哪兒?

To the post office.
去郵局。

a b c d e f g h i j k l m n o p q r s t u v w x y z

number 數字

/ ˈnʌmbə /

Can you read these numbers ?
你會讀這些數字嗎？

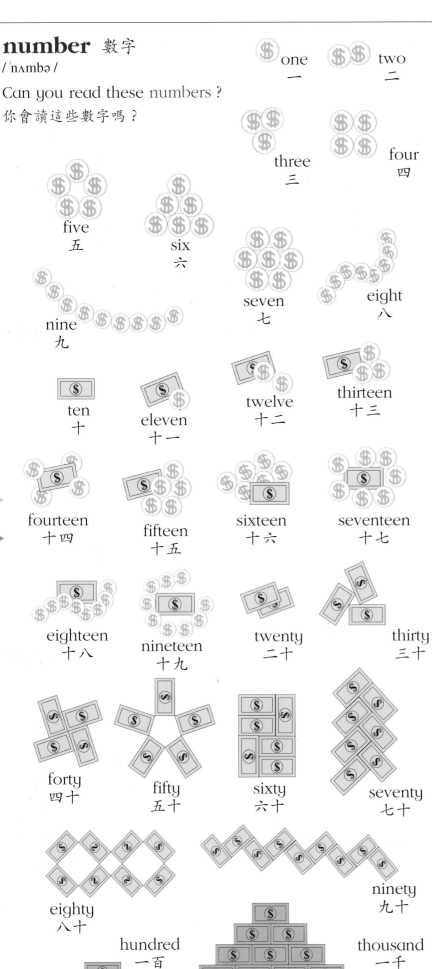

one 一

two 二

three 三

four 四

five 五

six 六

seven 七

eight 八

nine 九

ten 十

eleven 十一

twelve 十二

thirteen 十三

fourteen 十四

fifteen 十五

sixteen 十六

seventeen 十七

eighteen 十八

nineteen 十九

twenty 二十

thirty 三十

forty 四十

fifty 五十

sixty 六十

seventy 七十

eighty 八十

ninety 九十

hundred 一百

thousand 一千

nurse 護士

/ nɜːs /

What is Susan's mother ?
蘇珊的母親是幹甚麼的？

She's a nurse.
她是護士。

job

Oo

o'clock ...時

/ əˈklɒk /

The time now is eight o'clock in the morning.
現在的時間是上午八時。

time

October 十月
/ ɒkˈtəʊbə /

The weather is good in October.
十月份天氣很好。

`month`

off 從...離開
/ ɒf /

Mimi jumped off the table.
咪咪從桌子上跳了下來。

`where`

often 經常
/ ɒfn /

Hello
Hello
Hello...

My parrot often says "Hello".
我的鸚鵡經常說「你好」。

old 舊；年老
/ əʊld /

This is my old doll.
這是我的舊洋娃娃。

It's very dirty.
它很髒。

`opposite`

on 在...上
/ ɒn /

Where's my dress ?
我的裙子在哪兒？

It's on the bed.
在床上。

`where`

one 一
/ wʌn /

One from two is one.
二減一等於一。

`number`

onion 洋葱
/ ˈʌnɪən /

Onions can make you cry.
洋葱會使你流眼淚。

`vegetable`

open 打開
/ ˈəʊpən /

Why do you open your mouth ?
你為甚麼張開嘴？

opposite 對面；相反

/ ˈɒpəzɪt /

Black is the opposite of white.

黑是白的相反。

early
早

late
晚

fast
快

slow
慢

fat
胖

thin
瘦

ugly
醜陋

beautiful
美麗

clean
乾淨

dirty
骯髒

big
大

small
小

good
好

bad
壞

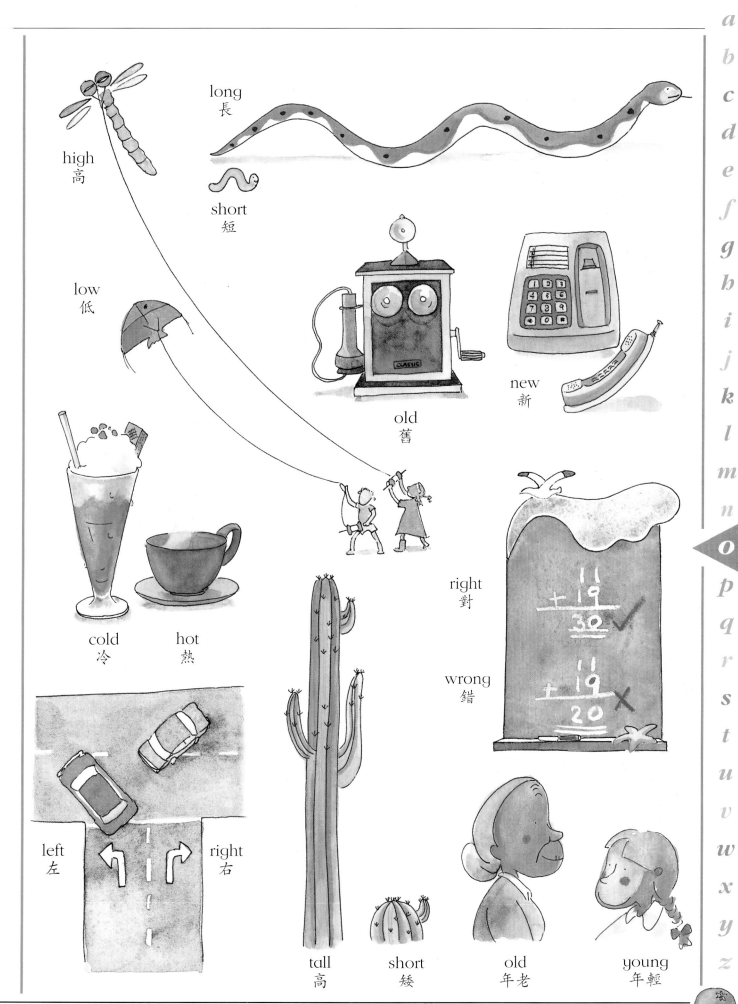

高

long
長

short
短

low
低

old
舊

new
新

cold
冷

hot
熱

right
對

wrong
錯

left
左

right
右

tall
高

short
矮

old
年老

young
年輕

or 或；還是
/ ɔː /

Do you want a banana or an apple ?
你要香蕉還是蘋果？

orange 橙；橙色
/ ˈɒrɪndʒ /

What colour is an orange ?
橙是甚麼顏色的？
Orange of course!
當然是橙色的。

`fruit`
`colour`

oven 烤爐
/ ˈʌvn /

What's this ?
這是甚麼？

This is an oven.
這是烤爐。

`kitchen`

our 我們的
/ ˈaʊə /

We like our teacher very much.
我們很喜歡我們的老師。

over 在...之上
/ ˈəʊvə /

There is a picture over the television.
電視機上面有一幅圖畫。

`where`

out 不在；在...外面
/ aʊt /

We'll eat out tonight.
我們今晚會在外面吃飯。

Yeah !
好極了！

`where`

owl 貓頭鷹
/ aʊl /

Owls can see very well at night.
貓頭鷹晚上視力很好。

`bird`

Pp

panda 熊貓
/ ˈpændə /

What animal is this ?
這是甚麼動物？
This is a panda.
這是熊貓。

zoo

paper 紙
/ ˈpeɪpə /

Can you do this with paper ?
你會用紙做這個嗎？

classroom

park 公園
/ pɑːk /

We often go to the park with our friends.
我們經常和朋友去公園玩。

swing
鞦韆

seesaw
蹺蹺板

tree
樹

slide
滑梯

flower
花

bench
長凳

pond
水池

grass
草

place

a b c d e f g h i j k l m n o p q r s t u v w x y z

parrot 鸚鵡
/ ˈpærət /

peacock 孔雀
/ ˈpiːkɒk /

What a beautiful peacock !
多麼漂亮的孔雀！

`bird`

What are you doing ?
你在做甚麼？
I'm talking to the parrots.
我在跟鸚鵡講話。 `bird`

pen 筆；鋼筆；原子筆
/ pen /

Where's my pen ?
我的筆在哪兒？
It's here.
在這裏。 `classroom`

pencil 鉛筆
/ ˈpensl /

Whose pencil is this ?
這是誰的鉛筆？
It's Paul's.
是保羅的。 `classroom`

people 人；人物
/ ˈpiːpl /

Who are these people ?
這些人是誰？

baby
嬰兒

boy
男孩

girl
女孩

woman
女人

man
男人

child
兒童

adult
成年人

piano 鋼琴
/ ˈpiænəʊ /

Do you play the piano ?
你會彈鋼琴嗎?
Yes, I do.
對,我會。

`music`

picture 圖畫;照片
/ ˈpɪktʃə /

How do you like this picture ?
你覺得這幅圖畫怎樣?
It's very beautiful.
它很好看。

`sitting-room`

pig 豬
/ pɪg /

There are many pigs on my father's farm.
我爸爸的農場養了很多豬。

`farm`

pigeon 鴿子
/ ˈpɪdʒɪn /

Do you like pigeons ?
你喜歡鴿子嗎?

Yes, very much.
對,我很喜歡。

`bird`

pillow 枕頭
/ ˈpɪləʊ /

Whose pillow is this ?
這是誰的枕頭?

`bedroom`

pineapple
/ ˈpaɪnæpl /

菠蘿;鳳梨

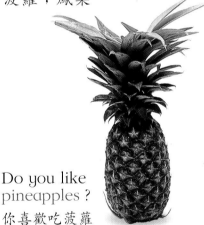

Do you like pineapples ?
你喜歡吃菠蘿嗎?

`fruit`

pink 粉紅色
/ pɪŋk /

This pink towel is mine.
這條粉紅色的毛巾是我的。

`colour`

a b c d e f g h i j k l m n o **p** q r s t u v w x y z

place 地方；位置
/ pleɪs /

I have been to many places.
我去過很多地方。

beach
海灘

cinema
電影院

department store
百貨公司

farm
農場

fire station
消防局

hospital
醫院

library
圖書館

market
市場

park
公園

police station
警察局

post office
郵局

restaurant
餐館

school
學校

CP SUPERMARKET

supermarket
超級市場

swimming-pool
游泳池

zoo
動物園

a b c d e f g h i j k l m n o p q r s t u v w x y z

plate 碟子；盤子
/ pleɪt /

What's on the plate ?
碟子上放着甚麼？
Some biscuits.
一些餅乾。

`dining-room`

play 玩
/ pleɪ /

What are you playing ?
你們在玩甚麼？

We're playing cat's cradle.
我們在玩翻繩兒。

please 請
/ pliːz /

Please give me a hand.
請你幫我一個忙。

OK, I'm coming.
好的，馬上來。

police station 警察局
/ pəˈliːs steɪʃn /

Have you been to the police station ?
你去過警察局嗎？
No, never.
從沒去過。

`place`

policeman 警察
/ pəˈliːsmən /

What is Peter's father ?
彼得的父親是幹甚麼的？
He's a policeman.
他是警察。

`job`

pond 水池；池塘
/ pɒnd /

There are some ducks swimming in the pond.
池塘裏有些鴨子在游泳。

`park`

post office 郵局
/ ˈpəʊst ɒfɪs /

Why do people go to the post office ?

人們為甚麼要去郵局？

place

postman 郵差
/ ˈpəʊstmən /

What is Henry's father ?

亨利的父親是幹甚麼的？

He's a postman.

他是郵差。

job

potato 馬鈴薯
/ pəˈteɪtəʊ /

Paul does not like potatoes.

保羅不喜歡吃馬鈴薯。

vegetable

pupil 學生
/ ˈpjuːpl /

There are hundreds of pupils in our school.

我們學校有幾百個學生。

classroom

puppet 木偶；布偶
/ ˈpʌpɪt /

Susan and Anne are playing with their puppets.

蘇珊和安妮在玩木偶。

toy

purple 紫色
/ ˈpɜːpl /

These are all purple.

這些都是紫色的。

colour

put 放置
/ pʊt /

Shall I put it here ?
是不是放在這裏？

put on
穿上

Qq

quilt 棉被；被子
/ kwɪlt /

Jack has a quilt on his bed in winter.

冬天時杰克的床上有被子。

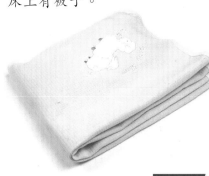

bedroom

a b c d e f g h i j k l m n o p q r s t u v w x y z

Rr

radio 收音機
/ ˈreɪdɪəʊ /

I bought a new radio yesterday.

我昨天買了一部新收音機。

sitting-room

read 讀；唸
/ riːd /

What are you reading ?

你在看甚麼？

I'm reading a storybook.

我在看故事書。

rain 雨；下雨
/ reɪn /

It has been raining for three days.

三天以來一直下雨。

weather

rectangle 長方形
/ ˈrektæŋgl /

What shapes are these ?

這些是甚麼形狀？

These are rectangles.

這些是長方形。

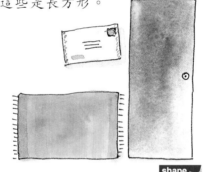

shape

red 紅色
/ red /

Apples, strawberries and cherries are all red.

蘋果、草莓和櫻桃都是紅色的。

colour

rainbow 彩虹
/ ˈreɪnbəʊ /

There is a beautiful rainbow in the sky.

天空有一道美麗的彩虹。

weather

restaurant 餐館
/ ˈrestrɒnt /

Jack and Helen went to a restaurant last night.

杰克和海倫昨晚去了一家餐館吃飯。

place

rice 米；米飯

/ raɪs /

John eats a lot of rice.
約翰吃很多飯。

food

right 對；右

/ raɪt /

Three and three make six.
三加三等於六。

Right !
對了！

opposite

robot 機械人

/ ˈrəʊbɒt /

What toys do you have ?
你有甚麼玩具？

I have many robots.
我有很多機械人。

rubber 橡皮擦

/ ˈrʌbə /

What's Paul looking for ?
保羅在找甚麼？

He's looking for his rubber.
他在找他的橡皮擦。

classroom

ruler 尺

/ ˈruːlə /

This is Henry's ruler.
這是亨利的尺。

classroom

run 跑

/ rʌn /

Peter ran to school yesterday morning.
昨天早上彼得跑回學校去。

toy

Ss

sad 悲傷；不高興

/ sæd /

Why are you so sad ?
你為甚麼這樣不高興？

Helen's angry with me.
海倫在生我的氣。

feeling
opposite

salt 鹽

/ sɔːlt /

We shouldn't eat too much salt.
我們不應該吃太多鹽。

Saturday 星期六

/ ˈsætədɪ /

Can you go to the cinema with me this Saturday ?
你這個星期六可以同我去看電影嗎？

week

a b c d e f g h i j k l m n o p q r s t u v w x y z

sausage 臘腸；香腸

/ ˈsɒsɪdʒ /

I'm hungry.

我肚子餓。

There are some sausages in the fridge.

冰箱裏有幾條香腸。

food

school 學校

/ skuːl /

There are five hundred pupils in our school.

我們學校有五百個學生。

place

season 季節

/ ˈsiːzn /

spring 春天

There are four seasons in a year.
一年有四季。

summer 夏天

autumn 秋天

winter 冬天

second 第二
/ ˈsekənd /

Where are my shorts?
我的短褲在哪兒？
In the second drawer.
在第二個抽屜裏面。

where

see 看見
/ siː /

What do you see?
你看見甚麼？
A UFO.
一個不明飛行物體。

seesaw 蹺蹺板
/ ˈsiːsɔː /

Where are Paul and Julie?
保羅和朱莉在哪兒？

They're playing on the seesaw.
他們在玩蹺蹺板。

park

September 九月
/ sepˈtembə /

School opens in September.
學校九月開課。

month

seven 七
/ ˈsevn /

A rainbow is made up of seven colours.
彩虹由七種顏色組成。

number

seventeen 十七
/ ˌsevnˈtiːn /

Ten and seven are seventeen.
十加七等於十七。

number

seventy 七十
/ ˈsevntɪ /

My English teacher gave me seventy marks.
我的英文老師給我七十分。

number

a b c d e f g h i j k l m n o p q r s t u v w x y z

shape 形狀
/ ʃeɪp /

What shapes are these ?
這些是甚麼形狀？

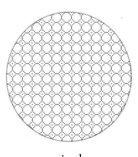

circle
圓形

square
正方形

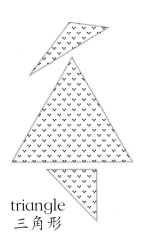

triangle
三角形

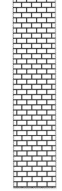

rectangle
長方形

she 她
/ ʃiː /

Who is she ?
她是誰？

She's my friend Amy.
她是我的朋友艾美。

ship 船
/ ʃɪp /

This ship can take thousands of people.
這隻船能夠載幾千人。

sheep 羊；綿羊
/ ʃiːp /

How many sheep are there ?
一共有多少隻羊？

There are three.
一共有三隻。

`farm`

shirt 襯衣
/ ʃɜːt /

Where's my shirt ?
我的襯衣在哪兒？

It's here.
在這裏。

`clothes`

shoe 鞋子
/ ʃuː /

What's Amy looking for ?
艾美在找甚麼？

She's looking for her shoes.
她在找她的鞋子。

`clothes`

short 短；矮
/ ʃɔːt /

I have short hair.
我有一頭短髮。

I have long hair.
我有一頭長髮。

opposite

shorts 短褲
/ ʃɔːts /

Who's the boy in shorts?
那個穿短褲的男孩是誰？
Sorry, I don't know.
對不起，我不知道。

clothes

shout 大叫；呼喊
/ ʃaʊt /

Julie!
朱莉！

Don't shout. Father is sleeping.
不要大叫，爸爸在睡覺。

sing 唱歌
/ sɪŋ /

...I sing this song for you...
...我為你唱這首歌...

singer 歌手
/ ˈsɪŋə /

Helen wants to be a singer.
海倫想當歌手。

job

sink 洗滌槽
/ sɪŋk /

There are some dirty plates in the sink.
洗滌槽裏有幾個骯髒的盤子。

kitchen

sister 姊妹
/ ˈsɪstə /

How many sisters does Jack have?
杰克有多少個姊妹？
One.
一個。

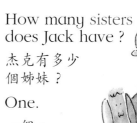

family

sit 坐
/ sɪt /

Why don't you sit down?
你為甚麼不坐下？

a b c d e f g h i j k l m n o p q r **s** t u v w x y z

sitting-room 客廳
/ ˈsɪtɪŋruːm /

picture
圖畫

fan
電風扇

door
門

window
窗

television
電視機

floor
地板

sofa
沙發

telephone
電話

This is our
sitting-room.
這是我們的
客廳。

vase
花瓶

cup
杯

radio
收音機

six 六
/ sɪks /

How many babies does the mother pig have ?

豬媽媽有多少隻小豬？

She has six.

她有六隻。

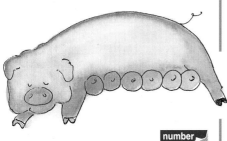

`number`

sky 天空
/ skaɪ /

I want to be a cloud in the sky.

我想做天空裏的一片雲。

sixteen 十六
/ sɪksˈtiːn /

Four fours are sixteen.

四乘四等於十六。

`number`

sleep 睡覺
/ sliːp /

Did you sleep well last night ?
你昨晚睡得好嗎？

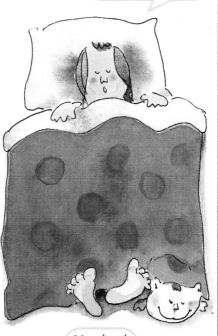

Not bad.
還可以。

slide 滑梯
/ slaɪd /

The children are playing on the slide.

孩子們在玩滑梯。

`park`

sixty 六十
/ ˈsɪkstɪ /

I am sixty years old.
我已經六十歲了。

`number`

slow 慢
/ sləʊ /

Don't be so slow.
不要這麼慢。

I'm tired.
我累了。

`opposite`

a b c d e f g h i j k l m n o p q r **s** t u v w x y z

small 小
/ smɔːl /

I can't put this pullover on. It's too small.
這件毛衣太小了，我穿不上。

`opposite`

soap 肥皂
/ səʊp /

Mary is washing her hands with soap.
瑪麗在用肥皂洗手。

`bathroom`

sock 襪子
/ sɒk /

Take off your socks.
把襪子脫下來。

No, I'm cold.
不，我很冷。

`clothes`

snake 蛇
/ sneɪk /

Are you afraid of snakes?
你怕蛇嗎？

Yes, very much.
是的，非常怕。

`zoo`

sofa 沙發
/ ˈsəʊfə /

Who's sleeping on the sofa?
誰在沙發上睡覺？

It's David.
是大衛。

`sitting-room`

snow 雪：下雪
/ snəʊ /

Oh, it's snowing again.
啊，又再下雪了。

`weather`

some 一些
/ sʌm /

Do you want some biscuits?
你想吃點餅乾嗎？

No, thanks.
不，謝謝。

sometimes 有時
/ ˈsʌmtaɪmz /

Do you play basketball ?
你打籃球嗎？
Yes, sometimes.
有時候打。

son 兒子
/ sʌn /

This is my son John.
這是我的兒子約翰。

soon 不久；很快
/ suːn /

When will the bus come ?
公共汽車甚麼時候才會來？
It'll soon come.
很快就會來。

sorry 對不起；抱歉
/ ˈsɒrɪ /

I'm sorry.
對不起。

It doesn't matter.
沒關係。

soup 湯
/ suːp /

What soup do we have today ?
我們今天喝甚麼湯？
Chicken soup.
雞湯。

sparrow 麻雀
/ ˈspærəʊ /

What bird is this ?
這是甚麼鳥？

This is a sparrow.
這是麻雀。

spoon 匙
/ spuːn /

There's only one spoon in the cupboard.
碗櫥裏只有一隻匙子。

a b c d e f g h i j k l m n o p q r **s** t u v w x y z

sport 運動

/ spɔːt /

What sports do you play ?

你參與哪些運動？

tennis
網球

badminton
羽毛球

basketball
籃球

football
足球

table tennis
乒乓球

cycling
騎自行車

volleyball
排球

swimming
游泳

spring 春天
/ sprɪŋ /

Which season do you like ?

你喜歡哪個季節 ?

I like spring.
我喜歡春天。

season

square 正方形
/ skweə /

How many squares are there ?

一共有多少個正方形 ?

Fourteen!

十四個 !

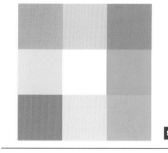

shape

story 故事
/ ˈstɔːrɪ /

Mother told us this story yesterday.

媽媽昨天給我們講了這個故事。

stand 站
/ stænd /

Why did you stand up, Paul ?

保羅，你為甚麼站起來 ?

Because...

因為...

stop 停止
/ stɒp /

We must stop at the red light.

我們必須在紅燈停下。

stove 爐子
/ stəʊv /

Julie, turn off the stove please.

朱莉，請把爐子關掉。

kitchen

sugar 糖
/ ʃʊgə /

The English take sugar with their tea.

英國人喝茶喜歡放糖。

a b c d e f g h i j k l m n o p q r **s** t u v w x y z

summer 夏天

/ ˈsʌmə /

We often go to the beach in summer.

我們夏天經常去海灘。

sun 太陽

/ sʌn /

Look, the sun is over us.

你看，太陽在我們頭上。

swallow 燕子

/ ˈswɒləʊ /

Have you ever seen a swallow?

你見過燕子嗎？

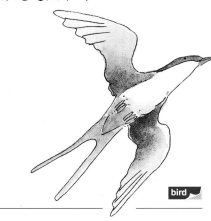

`bird`

`season`
`weather`

Sunday 星期日

/ ˈsʌndɪ /

What day is today?

今天是星期幾？

Today is Sunday.

今天是星期日。

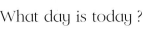

`week`

swan 天鵝

/ swɒn /

I want to be as beautiful as a swan.

我希望像天鵝一樣美麗。

`bird`

supermarket 超級市場

/ ˈsuːpəmaːkɪt /

What are you doing in the supermarket?

你在超級市場裏幹甚麼？

I'm looking for my mother.

我在找我媽媽。

`place`

sweet 糖果

/ swiːt /

Children must not eat too many sweets.

小孩子不可以吃太多糖果。

`food`

swim 游泳
/ swɪm /

Can you swim ?
你會游泳嗎？
Yes, I can.
我會。

swimming 游泳
/ ˈswɪmɪŋ /

swimming-pool
/ ˈswɪmɪŋpuːl /
游泳池

How often do you go to the swimming-pool ?
你多久去一次游泳池？

I like swimming very much.
我很喜歡游泳。

sport

place

swing 鞦韆
/ swɪŋ /

Anne is playing on a swing in the park.
安妮在公園裏蕩鞦韆。

park

Tt

table 桌子
/ ˈteɪbl /

What's on the table ?
桌子上放着甚麼？

It's my cup.
放着我的杯子。

dining-room

a b c d e f g h i j k l m n o p q r s t u v w x y z

table tennis 乒乓球
/ ˈteɪbl tenɪs /

Who's playing table tennis?
誰在打乒乓球？
Julie and Mary.
朱莉和瑪麗。

`sport`

take 拿；帶
/ teɪk /

When will you take me to the cinema?
你甚麼時候帶我去看電影？
Next week.
下星期。

take off
脫掉

talk 談話
/ tɔːk /

Can I talk to you?
我可以跟你談一談嗎？

Not now.
現在不行。

tall 高
/ tɔːl /

You are very tall.
你長得很高。

`opposite`

tap 水龍頭
/ tæp /

Turn off the tap, Jack.
杰克，把水龍頭關掉。

`kitchen`

taxi
/ ˈtæksɪ /

出租汽車；的士(方言)

Here comes a taxi.
出租汽車來了。

`vehicle`

tea 茶
/ tiː /

Would you like some tea?
你要不要喝點茶？

teacher 教師；老師
/ ˈtiːtʃə /

She is our English teacher.
她是我們的英語老師。

classroom

teddy bear 玩具熊
/ ˈtedɪ beə /

Whose teddy bear is this ?
這是誰的玩具熊？

It's Amy's.
是艾美的。

toy

telephone 電話
/ ˈtelɪfəʊn /

Do you have a telephone at home ?
你家裏有電話嗎？

sitting-room

television 電視；電視機
/ ˈtelɪvɪʒn /

What's on television ?
電視在做甚麼節目？
Well...
這個嘛…

sitting-room

tell 告訴
/ tel /

Tonight, I'll tell you the story of Ali Baba and the Forty Thieves.
今晚，我會給你們講阿里巴巴
與四十大盜的故事。

ten 十
/ ten /

Five and five are ten.
五加五等於十。

number

tennis 網球
/ ˈtenɪs /

Many people like playing tennis.
很多人喜歡打網球。

sport

a b c d e f g h i j k l m n o p q r s t u v w x y z

thank 感謝
/ θæŋk /

Thank you very much.
十分感謝你。

Not at all.
不要客氣。

that 那個
/ ðæt /

Who's that boy?
那個男孩是誰?

He's my friend Peter.
他是我的朋友彼得。

their 他們的;它們的
/ ðeə /

Jack and Mary are playing with their dogs.
杰克和瑪麗在跟他們的狗玩。

them 他們;它們
/ ðem /

Your shoes are very dirty. Go and wash them now.
你的鞋子很骯髒,馬上去把它們洗乾淨。

there 那裏
/ ðeə /

Where is Mimi?
咪咪在哪兒?

There she is.
她在那裏。

these 這些
/ ðiːz /

What are these?
這些是甚麼？

These are grapes.
這些是葡萄。

thin 瘦
/ θɪn /

John's mother is very thin.
約翰的母親很瘦。

opposite

thirsty 口渴
/ ˈθɜːstɪ /

Please give me a glass of water. I'm very thirsty.
請給我一杯水，我渴得很。

feeling

thirteen 十三
/ θɜːˈtiːn /

There are thirteen fishes.
一共有十三條魚。

number

they 他們；它們
/ ðeɪ /

Where are Paul and Henry?
保羅和亨利在哪兒？
They are at school.
他們在學校裏。

third 第三
/ θɜːd /

Anne lives on the third floor.
安妮住在三樓。

where

thirty 三十
/ ˈθɜːtɪ /

There are thirty days in April.
四月份有三十天。

number

this 這個
/ ðɪs /

I like this one.
我喜歡這個。
Do you ?
不是吧？

those 那些
/ ðəʊz /

What ?
甚麼？

Those ducks
are for you.
那些鴨子是給
你的。

thousand 一千
/ ˈθaʊznd /

This cup is a thousand years old.
這個杯子有一千年的歷史。

number

three 三
/ θriː /

I'm three
years old.
我今年三
歲。

number

Thursday 星期四
/ ˈθɜːzdɪ /

Did you see Jack last week ?
你上星期有沒有見過杰克？
Yes, I saw him on Thursday.
有，我上星期四見過他。

SUNDAY
Monday
Tuesday
Wednesday
Thursday
Friday
Saturday

week

tiger 老虎
/ ˈtaɪgə /

Many animals are afraid of tigers.
很多動物都怕老虎。

zoo

time 時間；時候
/ taɪm /

What time is it ?
現在幾點鐘？

morning 早上

seven fifteen
(a quarter past seven)
七時十五分

noon 中午

twelve o'clock
十二時

night 晚上

nine thirty
(half past nine)
九時三十分

evening 傍晚

six forty-five
(a quarter to seven)
六時四十五分

afternoon 下午

three twenty
(twenty past three)
三時二十分

tired 疲倦；累
/ ˈtaɪəd /

You look tired.
你看來很疲倦。

I walked three hours to come here.
我走了三小時的路才來到這裏。

feeling

today 今天
/ təˈdeɪ /

We have a wonderful time today.
我們今天玩得很高興。

when

toe 腳趾
/ təʊ /

How many toes do we have ?
我們有多少隻腳趾？
Ten.
十隻。

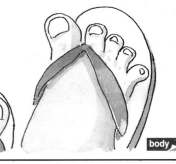

body

toilet 廁所；馬桶
/ ˈtɔɪlɪt /

Where's the toilet, please?
請問廁所在哪兒？
Over there.
在那裏。

tomato 番茄；西紅柿
/ təˈmɑːtəʊ /

There are three tomatoes in the fridge.
冰箱裏有三個番茄。

vegetable ▸

tomorrow 明天
/ təˈmɒrəʊ /

Tomorrow is Sunday. I'll go to the beach with Jack.
明天是星期日，我會同杰克去海灘。

when ▸

tonight 今晚
/ təˈnaɪt /

Can I have dinner with you tonight?
我今晚可以同你吃晚飯嗎？

when ▸

tooth 牙齒
/ tuːθ /

I have a tooth.
我有一隻牙齒。
I have two teeth.
我有兩隻牙齒。

face ▸

toothbrush 牙刷
/ ˈtuːθbrʌʃ /

Do you have a toothbrush?
你有牙刷嗎？

bathroom ▸

toothpaste 牙膏
/ ˈtuːθpeɪst /

We are out of toothpaste.
我們的牙膏用完了。

bathroom ▸

towel 毛巾
/ ˈtaʊəl /

This towel is very big, isn't it?
這條毛巾很大，不是嗎？

bathroom ▸

toy 玩具
/ tɔɪ /

What toys do you have ?
你有甚麼玩具 ?

balls
球

cards
紙牌

balloons
氣球

robots
機械人

chess
棋

dolls
洋娃娃

blocks
積木

teddy bears
玩具熊

puppets
布偶

video game
電視遊戲

train 火車
/ treɪn /

Julie and Mary go to school by train.
朱莉和瑪麗坐火車上學。

vehicle

tram 電車
/ træm /

If you go to Hong Kong, you will see a tram like this.
如果你去香港，就會看到這種電車。

vehicle

tree 樹
/ tri: /

What tree is this?   This is an apple tree.
這是甚麼樹？   這是蘋果樹。

park

triangle 三角形
/ ˈtraɪæŋgl /

How many triangles are there?

一共有多少個
三角形？

Nine!

九個！

shape

trousers 褲子
/ ˈtraʊzəz /

That monkey has put my trousers on.
那隻猴子穿上了我的褲子。

clothes

Tuesday 星期二
/ ˈtjuːzdɪ /

I'll see Amy on Tuesday.
我星期二約了艾美。

week

twelve 十二
/ twelv /

Three fours are twelve.
三乘四等於十二。

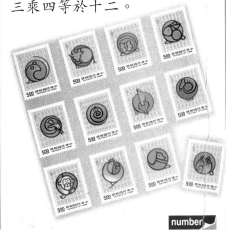

number

twenty 二十
/ ˈtwentɪ /

Four fives are twenty.
四乘五等於二十。

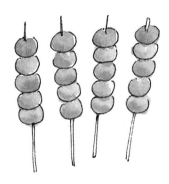

`number`

two 二
/ tuː /

Susan eats
two apples a day.
蘇珊每天吃兩個蘋果。 `number`

Uu

ugly 難看；醜陋
/ ˈʌglɪ /

You look ugly !
你很難看！

What ?
甚麼？

`opposite`

under 在...之下
/ ˈʌndə /

Where's Dudu ?
嘟嘟在哪兒？
He's under the chair.
他在椅子下面。

`where`

up 往上
/ ʌp /

David wants to climb up
the slide.
大衛要爬到滑梯上去。

`where`

us 我們
/ ʌs /

Will somebody help us ?
會有人救我們嗎？

Vv

vase 花瓶
/ vɑːz /

A beautiful vase needs
beautiful flowers.

漂亮的花瓶需要
漂亮的花朵。

`sitting-room`

a
b
c
d
e
f
g
h
i
j
k
l
m
n
o
p
q
r
s
t
u
v
w
x
y
z

vegetable 蔬菜
/ ˈvedʒtəbl /

Do you like these vegetables ?
你喜歡吃這些蔬菜嗎？

cucumber
黃瓜

corn
玉米

lettuce
生菜

potatoes
馬鈴薯

onions
洋蔥

carrots
胡蘿蔔

mushrooms
蘑菇

tomatoes
番茄

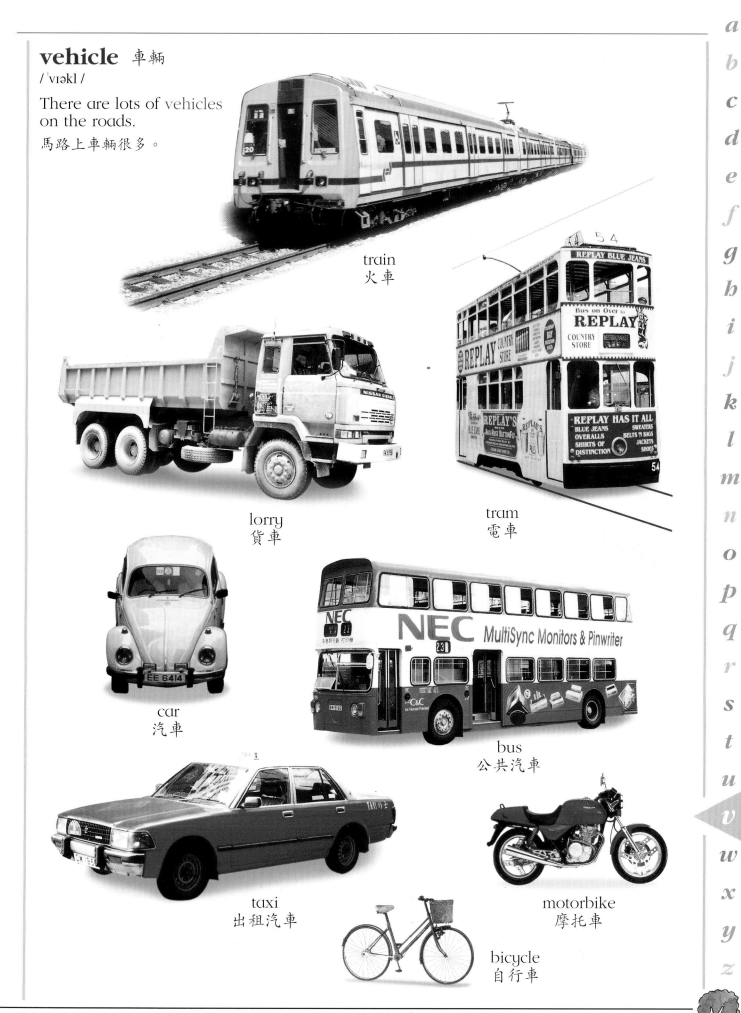

vehicle 車輛

/ˈvɪəkl /

There are lots of vehicles on the roads.

馬路上車輛很多。

train
火車

lorry
貨車

tram
電車

car
汽車

bus
公共汽車

taxi
出租汽車

motorbike
摩托車

bicycle
自行車

video game 電視遊戲
/ ˈvɪdɪəʊ ɡeɪm /

Video games are bad
for your eyes.
電視遊戲對眼睛有害。

`toy`

violin 小提琴
/ vaɪəˈlɪn /

Can you play the violin ?
你會拉小提琴嗎？

`music`

volleyball 排球
/ ˈvɒlɪbɔːl /

What are they doing ?
他們在做甚麼？
They're playing volleyball.
他們在打排球。

`sport`

Ww

walk 走；步行
/ wɔːk /

You walk
too slow.
你走得太慢。

You walk
too fast.
你走得太
快了。

want 想要
/ wɒnt /

What do you want for
Christmas ?
聖誕節你想要甚麼禮物？

I want a bicycle.
我想要一輛自行車。

wash 洗
/ wɒʃ /

What's Helen doing ?
海倫在做甚麼？
She's washing her clothes.
她在洗衣服。

water 水
/ ˈwɔːtə /

Fish live in water.

魚在水裏生活。

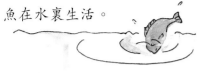

watermelon 西瓜
/ ˈwɔːtəmelən /

What's this ?

這是甚麼 ?

This is a watermelon.

這是西瓜。

fruit ►

we 我們
/ wiː /

Where are we ?
我們在哪兒 ?
We're in the sky.
我們在天空中。

weather 天氣
/ ˈweðə /

The weather was very bad yesterday.

昨天天氣很差。

cloud 雲

rainbow 彩虹

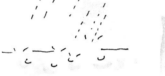

rain 雨

sun 太陽

snow 雪

wind 風

Wednesday 星期三
/ ˈwenzdɪ /

I was at home last Wednesday.

上個星期三我在家。

week ►

week 星期；週
/ wi:k /

There are seven days in a week.

一星期有七天。

Monday
星期一

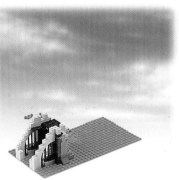

Tuesday
星期二

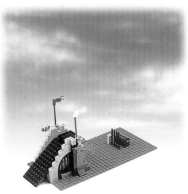

Wednesday
星期三

Thursday
星期四

Friday
星期五

Saturday
星期六

Sunday
星期日

well 健康；出色
/ wel /

Jack played football very well yesterday.

杰克昨天踢足球踢得很出色。

opposite

what 甚麼
/ wɒt /

What do you see ?

你看見甚麼？

when 甚麼時候
/ wen /

When will you give the flowers to Henry ?
你甚麼時候會把花送給亨利？
Tomorrow.
明天。

today 今天

tomorrow 明天

yesterday 昨天

tonight 今晚

where 甚麼地方
/ weə /

Where are they ?
它們在哪兒？

on 在...上

off 從...離開

under 在...之下

over 在...之上

in 在...裏面

out 在...外面

up 往上

down 往下

last 最後

third 第三

second 第二

first 第一

which 哪個
/ wɪtʃ /

Which do you want ?
你要哪個？

I want an apple.
我要蘋果。

white 白色
/ waɪt /

What colour is milk ?
牛奶是甚麼顏色的？

It's white.
是白色的。

colour

why 為甚麼
/ waɪ /

Why did the apple come down on my head ?
這蘋果為甚麼會掉在我的頭上？

who 誰
/ huː /

Who are you ?
你是誰？

I'm Superman.
我是超人。

whose 誰的
/ huːz /

It's Julie's.
是朱莉的。

Whose letter is this ?
這是誰的信？

will 將會
/ wɪl /

Will Mother be angry ?
媽媽會生氣嗎？

wind 風
/ ˌwɪnd /

We can't stand the wind.
我們受不了這風。

weather

window 窗
/ ˈwɪndəʊ /

Julie opened the window.
朱莉把窗打開了。

sitting-room

wrong 錯
/ rɒŋ /

You're wrong. Two and two are four.
你錯了，二加二等於四。

opposite

winter 冬天
/ ˈwɪntə /

Do you go swimming in winter?
你冬天去游泳嗎？

season

Xx

xylophone 木琴
/ ˈzaɪləfəʊn /

You play the xylophone very well.
你彈木琴彈得很好。

Thank you.
謝謝。

music

woman 女人
/ ˈwʊmən /

There's a woman over there.
那邊有一個女人。

No, there are two women.
不，有兩個女人才對。

people

write 寫
/ raɪt /

What are you writing?
你在寫甚麼？

I'm writing a letter.
我在寫信。

a b c d e f g h i j k l m n o p q r s t u v **w** **x** y z

Yy

year 年
/ jɜː /

December 31 is the last day of the year.

十二月三十一日是一年的最後一天。

yellow 黃色
/ ˈjeləʊ /

Lemons are yellow.

檸檬是黃色的。

`colour`

you 你
/ juː /

Do you like this dictionary?
你喜歡這本字典嗎?

young 年輕
/ jʌŋ /

Susan's mother looks very young.

蘇珊的媽媽看來很年輕。

`opposite`

your 你的
/ jɔː /

Is this your fish?

這是你的魚嗎?

No, it's John's.

不,它是約翰的。

Zz

yesterday 昨天
/ ˈjestədɪ /

Why didn't you come yesterday?

你昨天怎麼沒來?

I was ill.
我病了。

`when`

zebra 斑馬
/ ˈziːbrə /

A zebra looks like a horse.

斑馬看起來很像馬。

`zoo`

ZOO 動物園
/ zu: /

Have you been to
the zoo ?
你去過動物園嗎？

elephant
象

bear
熊

monkey
猴子

zebra
斑馬

tiger
老虎

panda
熊貓

kangaroo
袋鼠

lion
獅子

snake
蛇

WELCOME

crocodile
鱷魚

place

a
b
c
d
e
f
g
h
i
j
k
l
m
n
o
p
q
r
s
t
u
v
w
x
y
z

Additional Words 附加字詞

a, an / ə, ən / 一個

Ali Baba / ˌælɪˈbɑːbə / 阿里巴巴

all / ɔːl / 全部

am / əm / be 的另一形式

Amy / ˈeɪmɪ / 艾美

Anne / æn / 安妮

are / ɑː / be 的另一形式

at / æt / 在...

Australia / ɒˈstreɪljə / 澳洲

be / bɪ / 是

been / biːn / be 的另一形式

best / best / 最好的

bought / bɔːt / buy 的另一形式

build / bɪld / 建造

but / bʌt / 但是

buy / baɪ / 買

can't / kɑːnt / = cannot

cherry / ˈtʃerɪ / 櫻桃

Christmas / ˈkrɪsməs / 聖誕節

could / kʊd / can 的另一形式

dad / dæd / 爸爸

David / ˈdeɪvɪd / 大衛

did / dɪd / do 的另一形式

didn't / ˈdɪdnt / = did not

does / dʌz / do 的另一形式

dollar / ˈdɒlə / 元

don't / dəʊnt / = do not

Dudu / ˈduːduː / 嘟嘟

ever / ˈevə / 曾經

every / ˈevrɪ / 每一

fastest / ˈfɑːstɪst / 最快的

favourite / ˈfeɪvərɪt / 最喜愛的

feet / fiːt / foot 的複數

fifth / fɪfθ / 第五

fool / fuːl / 傻瓜

for / fə / 給

fourteenth / ˈfɔːˈtiːnθ / 第十四

fourth / fɔːθ / 第四

from / frəm / 從...

geese / giːs / goose 的複數

giraffe / dʒɪˈrɑːf / 長頸鹿

God / gɒd / 上帝

goes / gəʊz / go 的另一形式

got / gɒt / get 的另一形式

grandpa / ˈgrænpə / 爺爺

had / hæd / have 的另一形式

half / hɑːf / 一半

has / hæz / have 的另一形式

haven't / ˈhævnt / = have not

he's / hiːz / = he is

Helen / ˈhelɪn / 海倫

Henry / ˈhenrɪ / 亨利

homework / ˈhəʊmwɜːk / 家庭作業

Hong Kong / ˈhɒŋ ˈkɒŋ / 香港

I'll / aɪl / = I will

I'm / aɪm / = I am

I've / aɪv / = I have

is / ɪz / be 的另一形式

it's / ɪts / = it is

Jack / dʒæk / 杰克

John / dʒɒn / 約翰

Julie / ˈdʒuːlɪ / 朱莉

know / nəʊ / 知道

live / lɪv / 居住

lot / lɒt / 很多

made / meɪd / make 的另一形式

many / ˈmenɪ / 很多

mark / mɑːk / 分數

Mary / ˈmærɪ / 瑪麗

men / men / man 的複數

mice / maɪs / mouse 的複數

Mimi / ˈmɪmɪ / 咪咪

mine / maɪn / 屬於我的

much / mʌtʃ / 很多

mum / mʌm / 媽媽

need / niːd / 需要

neither / ˈnaɪðə / 兩者都不...

no / nəʊ / 不；沒有

not / nɒt / 不

of / əv / ...的

OK / əʊˈkeɪ / 好

past / pɑːst / 過了

Paul / pɔːl / 保羅

pay / peɪ / 付款

Peter / ˈpiːtə / 彼得

pound / paʊnd / 磅

pullover / ˈpʊləʊvə / 套頭毛衣

quarter / ˈkwɔːtə / 四分之一

race / reɪs / 比賽

ride / raɪd / 騎

Saint Valentine's Day

　　/ seɪnt ˈvælətaɪnz deɪ / 情人節

saw / sɔː / see 的另一形式

shall / ʃəl / 將會

she's / ʃiːz / = she is

should / ʃʊd / shall 的另一形式

shouldn't / ˈʃʊdnt / = should not

so / səʊ / 很

somebody / ˈsʌmbədɪ / 某人

song / sɒŋ / 歌曲

storey / ˈstɔːrɪ / 層

superman / ˈsuːpəmæn / 超人

Susan / ˈsuːzn / 蘇珊

teeth / tiːθ / tooth 的複數

tenth / tenθ / 第十

thank you / ˈθæŋ kjʊ / 謝謝

the / ðə / 這；那

there's / ðeəz / = there is

they're / ðeɪə / = they are

thief / θiːf / 小偷

thieves / θiːvz / thief 的複數

to / tuː / 往；至

too / tuː / 太過

try / traɪ / 嘗試

turn off / ˈtɜːn ɒf / 關

turn on / ˈtɜːn ɒn / 開

UFO / juːefˈəʊ / 不明飛行物體

use / juːz / 用

very / ˈverɪ / 非常

was / wɒz / be 的另一形式

we're / wɪə / = we are

went / went / go 的另一形式

were / wɜː / be 的另一形式

what's / wɒts / = what is

where's / weəz / = where is

who's / huːz / = who is

with / wɪð / 和...一起

women / ˈwɪmɪn / woman 的複數

won't / wəʊnt / = will not

wonderful / ˈwʌndəfl / 很好的

world / wɜːld / 世界

would / wʊd / will 的另一形式

wow / waʊ / 哇！

yes / jes / 是

you're / jʊə / = you are

yours / jɔːz / 屬於你的

Special thanks to
Ms Julia So
Ms Liu Tsz Yau
Mr Chan Hon Piu
Mr Chan Kit
Mr Laurence Lee
Mr Yeung Chi Kin
for their kind help in producing this book.

小兒童英文彩圖字典
Children's Picture Dictionary

繪圖 **Illustrator:**	Shirley Wong 王秀蘭
編輯 **Editor:**	Lau Yung Keung 劉勇強
設計 **Designer:**	Leung Siu Hong 梁兆康
正稿 **Artist:**	Muk Kwok Man 穆國敏
Publisher:	The Commercial Press (Hong Kong) Ltd. 2D Finnie St., Quarry Bay, Hong Kong
Printer:	South Sea International Press Ltd. 3/F Yip Cheung Centre, 10 Fung Yip Street, Chaiwan, Hong Kong
Edition/Impression:	1st Edition/1st Impression ©1995 The Commercial Press (Hong Kong) Ltd. ISBN 962 07 0171 2

All inquiries should be directed to:

The Commercial Press (Hong Kong) Ltd.
Kiu Ying Building, 2D Finnie Street, Quarry Bay, Hong Kong